Cat-ographies

American Shorthairs
Pioneers

by Jessica Rudolph

Consultant: Virginia Wight, M.D.
President, National American Shorthair Club
www.ashclub.org

Credits

Cover and Title Page, © Richard Katris/Chanan Photography; TOC, © Richard Katris/Chanan Photography; 4, © Courtesy National Archives/Kimberlee Hewitt; 5L, © White House Photo Office/Susan Sterner; 5R, © Paul Morse; 6, © Image Asset Management Ltd./SuperStock; 7, © Kenneth H. Thomas/Photo Researchers, Inc.; 8T, © North Wind Picture Archives/Alamy; 8B, © Johan De Meester/Arterra Picture Library/Alamy; 9, © Callalloo Francais/Pixmac; 10, © Barbara O'Brien Photography; 11L, © Richard Katris/Chanan Photography; 11R, © Richard Katris/Chanan Photography; 12TL, © J-L Klein & M-L Hubert/Bios/Photolibrary; 12TR, © Richard Katris/Chanan Photography; 12BL, © Richard Katris/Chanan Photography; 12BR, © Richard Katris/Chanan Photography; 13T, © Richard Katris/Chanan Photography; 13B, © Richard Katris/Chanan Photography; 14, © Japack/age fotostock; 15, © Frank Nash/Alamy; 16L, © Richard Katris/Chanan Photography; 16R, © Richard Katris/Chanan Photography; 17, © Barbara O'Brien Photography; 18T, © Eunice Pearcy/Animals Animals Enterprises; 18B, © MIXA/SuperStock; 19, © Nao Imai/Aflo Foto Agency/Photolibrary; 20, © Barbara O'Brien Photography; 21, © White House Photo Office/Paul Morse; 22, © Richard Katris/Chanan Photography; 23, © Tamila Aspen/Shutterstock.

Publisher: Kenn Goin
Senior Editor: Lisa Wiseman
Creative Director: Spencer Brinker
Design: Dawn Beard Creative
Photo Researcher: Omni-Photo Communications, Inc.

Library of Congress Cataloging-in-Publication Data

Rudolph, Jessica.
  American shorthairs : pioneers / by Jessica Rudolph.
    p. cm. — (Cat-ographies)
  Includes bibliographical references and index.
  ISBN-13: 978-1-61772-143-4 (library binding)
  ISBN-10: 1-61772-143-3 (library binding)
  1. American shorthair cat—Juvenile literature. I. Title.
  SF449.A45R83 2011
  636.8'22—dc22
                    2010037155

For more information, write to Bearport Publishing Company, Inc., 101 Fifth Avenue, Suite 6R, New York, New York 10003. Printed in the United States of America in North Mankato, Minnesota.

122010
10810CGD

10 9 8 7 6 5 4 3 2 1

Contents

First Cat

From 2001 to 2009, a very special four-legged furball lived in the White House with President George W. Bush and his family. India, a black American shorthair, was a very important member of the **First Family**.

India in the White House

Living in the White House was a great place for doing what India liked to do best—play hide-and-seek. The 132 rooms provided her with lots of great places to hide. It also made it very hard for her owners to find her. When she was done playing, the little black cat would curl up under a bed in one of the 16 White House bedrooms. Like all American shorthairs, India was a very special kind of cat.

India, shown here with President Bush's wife, Laura, moved into the White House in 2001. Sadly, India passed away in January 2009 at the age of 18.

President Bush's daughters, Barbara (left) and Jenna (right), pose with India at Jenna's wedding.

Barbara Bush named India after Rubén Sierra, a Texas Ranger baseball player who was nicknamed "El Indio." India's family also called her "Willie" and "Kitty."

Master Mousers

While India was a **pampered** pet, her **ancestors** were used to working very hard. The American shorthairs of today are related to cats brought to North America on ships by **pioneers** from Europe hundreds of years ago. Records show that one group from England, the Pilgrims, brought some shorthaired cats with them on their ship called the *Mayflower*.

Where American Shorthairs Came From

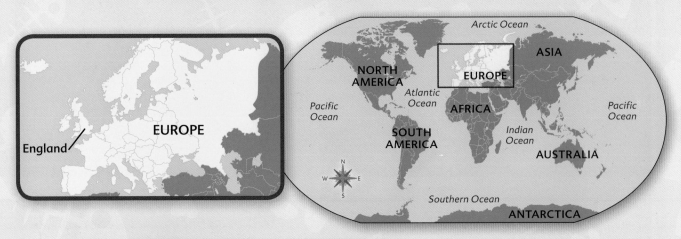

The Pilgrims left England on the *Mayflower* (shown here) in 1620, and landed in what is today Plymouth, Massachusetts. They were just one group of pioneers who brought cats with them when they came to North America hundreds of years ago.

While aboard the pioneers' ships, the shorthaired cats had a tough job—killing **rodents**! Before leaving for America, the ships were packed with lots of food. Rats and mice would sneak on for a meal, and the ships would leave with them still aboard. The cats protected the food during the trip by eating these sneaky rodents.

The cats that came from Europe to North America on ships may have looked like this one.

Cats that hunt rodents are called **mousers**. American shorthair cats are among the best mousers in the world.

All-American Cats

Once in America, pioneers such as the Pilgrims built farms. Just like the pioneers, the cats that came from Europe worked hard. On the farms, the cats hunted rodents, while also guarding the food found in homes, barns, and in the field.

A group of Pilgrims building a farmhouse in Plymouth, Massachusetts

There are lots of places on a farm where rodents can steal food.

These farm cats spent a lot of time outside. Over the years, they **adapted** to hunting in the harsh weather of North America. How? The cats' coats got thicker, which protected them from the cold and rain. The animals also grew larger and stronger. This made it easier for them to catch mice.

By the 1800s, people started calling the cats from Europe "shorthairs," and then "domestic shorthairs." In the 1960s, the **breed**'s name was changed to American shorthair, ASH for short, to honor its all-American past. This new name also separated them from other shorthaired cats that weren't **purebreds**.

While hunting, cats use their sense of smell. When they smell a rodent, they stay still until it comes near. They then pounce, killing the animal by biting its neck. This American shorthair cat is getting ready to pounce.

Strong Body, Cute Face

Today, most American shorthairs live indoors. They still, however, have the same strong hunting **instincts** as their ancestors. While most homes are no longer full of rodents, ASH cats have no problem chasing after other unwanted visitors such as spiders and flies.

These cats are also still known for their strong, hunter-like bodies. They can weigh 6 to 15 pounds (2.7 to 6.8 kg), with most of that weight due to the animal's large muscles. In fact, American shorthairs are more muscular than many other breeds.

As their name suggests, American shorthairs have short hair. It is full, shiny, and thick. Because their hair is short, the cats have to be **groomed** only about once a week.

This pet owner is combing her ASH cat's hair. Just like their ancestors, today's ASH cats have coats that protect them from the rain and harsh weather.

Pet owners today are usually not looking for cats that like to hunt or are strong. They are looking for cute cats—and American shorthairs certainly fit the bill. Their large, wide-spaced eyes give them a sweet look. Some people think male American shorthairs are even cuter than the females. The males have bigger **jowls**, which make them look like they have chubby cheeks!

The cheeks of a male ASH cat (below) are chubby compared to those of a female ASH cat (right).

A Cat of Many Colors

The American shorthair's short, thick coat comes in more than 80 combinations of colors and **patterns**. Some of these cats can be one solid color such as black, white, blue, red, or cream. Other cats can be a combination of two colors, such as black and white. Still others can come in patterns such as **calico**, **tortoiseshell**, or **tabby**.

A black ASH

A calico ASH

A tortoiseshell ASH

A red tabby ASH

The most well-known American shorthair pattern today is the silver classic tabby. A cat with this pattern has black markings that occur in a bull's eye shape on each of its sides, along with stripes down its back and tail.

American shorthairs' eyes come in a rainbow of colors, including gold, copper, green, or blue. They can also be odd-eyed. This means that each eye is a different color.

More than one third of American shorthairs are silver classic tabbies.

The Just-Right Cat

Owners of American shorthairs not only love their pets' looks, they love their **personalities**, too. These cats are easygoing and gentle. They aren't couch potatoes, and they're not too active. They're just the right mix.

American shorthairs are affectionate animals.

Although they like to cuddle and be held, they'll do it only if it's their idea. Some American shorthairs don't like being picked up so it's best for people to wait for them to jump onto their laps or into their arms.

ASH cats are independent. If their human families aren't around, they'll find ways to keep busy.

American shorthairs sometimes behave like dogs. They greet their owners at the door when they come home and follow them from room to room.

Silent Language

American shorthairs are known for being quiet. They don't meow often or too loudly. Instead, they find other ways to **communicate**. For example, ASH cats are famous for their silent meows. Sometimes a cat will walk up to its owner and open its mouth. Yet no sound will come out. What is the cat saying? It might be "I'm hungry" or "Pay attention to me."

This cat is swatting an imaginary toy.

The silent meow

ASH cats love to play with toys so much that if they can't find any, their owners may find their cats happily playing with something that isn't there.

An American shorthair may also communicate by nibbling its owner's bare toes. This love bite could be followed by a grin or a wag of the tail. This time, the cat is probably saying, "Let's play!" After spending lots of time with their cats, most owners eventually figure out their pets' silent language.

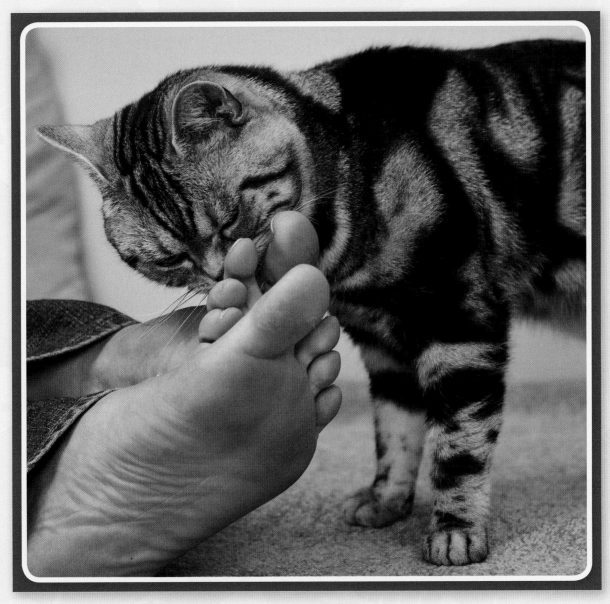

An American shorthair nibbling its owner's toes

Shorthair Kittens

For anyone who's seen an American shorthair kitten up close, it's love at first sight. They are that cute! When they're first born, they're tiny, helpless balls of fur. In just a few days, though, they can crawl. At three weeks old, they start to stand.

Most mother ASH cats have about three to four kittens. However, some have more.

ASH kittens

Kittens grow razor-sharp teeth about a month after they're born. They use them, too! They bite, wrestle, kick, and chase the other kittens. Nobody gets hurt, though. They're just play fighting. This is how they learn to get along with other cats.

Playing helps keep kittens' hunting instincts sharp.

To keep American shorthairs safe from animals that could harm them or from getting hit by a car, breeders recommend keeping them inside at all times. If an owner wants to take his or her pet outside, then the cat should be kept under constant supervision.

A New Family

When they're three to four months old, American shorthairs are ready to become part of a human family. Learning the rules of their new home is easy for ASH cats. For example, they like to climb to high places but can be trained to stay off counters and tables. They can even be taught to **fetch** toys or sit for a treat.

The American shorthair is one of the healthiest cat breeds. If they are kept indoors and taken for regular checkups with a **veterinarian,** they can live for 15 to 20 years.

One thing these lovable cats don't need to be taught, however, is how to fit in with other family members. From the start they'll get along well with children, other cats, and even dogs. New American shorthair owners will quickly learn that these adorable cats make perfect pets.

President Bush's cat, India, got along great with Barney (left) and Miss Beazley (right), Scottish terriers that also lived in the White House and were pets of the First Family.

American Shorthairs at a Glance

Weight:	Males weigh 10–15 pounds (4.5–6.8 kg); females weigh 6–9 pounds (2.7–4 kg)
Height:	Males are about 12–14 inches (30.5–35.6 cm) tall; females are about 10–12 inches (25.4–30.5 cm) tall
Coat Hair:	Short, thick, shiny, designed to protect from rain or harsh weather
Colors:	More than 80 combinations of colors and patterns, including solid colors such as black, white, and blue; patterns include silver classic tabby, calico, and tortoiseshell
Continent: of Origin:	Europe
Life Span:	15–20 years
Personality:	Friendly, independent, intelligent, good-natured, quiet; gets along well with other animals and children
Special Physical Characteristics:	A hardy medium-size body; muscular legs; a large, broad head with a full-cheeked face in the males; strong jaws; a thick, short coat

Glossary

adapted (uh-DAP-tid) changed over time to survive in an environment

ancestors (AN-sess-turz) family members who lived long ago

breed (BREED) a type of a certain animal

calico (KAL-i-koh) having a coat that has large, solid patches of two colors such as black and red along with large patches of white

communicate (kuh-MYOO-nuh-kate) to share information, ideas, feelings, and thoughts

fetch (FECH) to go after something and then bring it back

First Family (FURST FAM-uh-lee) the family of the President of the United States

groomed (GROOMD) combed and cleaned

instincts (IN-stingkts) knowledge and ways of acting that an animal is born with and does not have to learn

jowls (JOULZ) layers of loose skin on the cheeks, jaw, or throat

mousers (MOUSS-urz) cats that are good at catching mice and rats

pampered (PAM-purd) treated with much care and attention

patterns (PAT-urnz) sets of markings, such as stripes or spots, that are shown over and over

personalities (*pur*-suh-NAL-uh-teez) the character traits that make people or animals act the way they do

pioneers (*pye*-uh-NEERZ) people who go to live in a place that is not yet settled

purebreds (PYOOR-breds) animals whose parents, grandparents, and other ancestors are all the same kind of animal

rodents (ROH-duhnts) a group of animals with large front teeth that includes rats, mice, squirrels, and chipmunks

tabby (TAB-ee) having a coat with a specific repetition of markings such as stripes or spots

tortoiseshell (TOR-tuhss-*shell*) having a solid-colored coat that has black and red patches; the coat has markings like those found on a tortoise's shell

veterinarian (*vet*-ur-uh-NER-ee-uhn) a doctor who cares for animals

Index

Bibliography

Morris, Desmond. *Cat Breeds of the World: A Complete Illustrated Encyclopedia.* New York: Viking (1999).

Siegal, Mordecai, ed. *The Cat Fanciers' Association Complete Cat Book.* New York: HarperResource (2004).

www.ashclub.org

Read More

Furstinger, Nancy. *American Shorthair Cats.* Edina, MN: Checkerboard Books (2005).

Mattern, Joanne. *The American Shorthair Cat.* Mankato, MN: Capstone Press (2003).

Perkins, Wendy. *American Shorthair Cats.* Mankato, MN: Capstone Press (2008).

Learn More Online

To learn more about American shorthair cats, visit
www.bearportpublishing.com/Cat-ographies

About the Author

Jessica Rudolph has edited many books about animals. She lives in Phoenix, Arizona, where she volunteers at a shelter for cats and dogs.